THOUGH WAR
BREAK OUT

For Sharon —
Do not lose heart.
Everything good to you.

—Brad

ALSO BY BRAD DAVIS

Short List of Wonders

Winner of the 2005 Sunken Garden Poetry Contest

THOUGH WAR BREAK OUT

Book One of
Opening King David

Poems by

Brad Davis

Antrim House

Simsbury, Connecticut

Library of Congress Cataloging-in-Publication Data

Davis, Brad, 1952-
  Though war break out : poems / by Brad Davis.— 1st ed.
    p. cm. — (Opening King David ; bk. 1)
  Includes bibliographical references.
  ISBN 0-9762091-7-9 (alk. paper)
1. Bible. O.T. Psalms—Paraphrases, English. 2. David,
King of Israel—Poetry. 3. Religious poetry, American.
I. Title II. Series: Davis, Brad, 1952- . Opening King
David ; bk. 1.

  PS3604.A5556T48 2005
  811'.6—dc22
                                        2005013097

Cover print (*David in the Valley of Elah*) by Barry Moser

Book title: from Psalm 27:3

Author photo: Bill Pratt

Antrim House

www.antrimhousebooks.com

860.217.0023

for Deb, of course, and John

ACKNOWLEDGEMENTS

Thanks to the editors of the following journals, in which the poems listed below first appeared:

Ascent: "Eucharist"

Tar River Poetry: "Neighbor as Theologian"

Main Street Rag: "Answer Me," "Crossing the Williamsburg Bridge," "So"

And special thanks to these teachers and friends: D. A. Stevens, Ann Ferguson, David Wojahn, Jonathan Holden, Jack Myers, Syd Lea, Gray Jacobik, Bob Cording, Barry Moser, and Bill Pratt.

CONTENTS

CONTENTS

"These conjectures as to why God does what He does are probably of no more value than my dog's ideas of what I am up to when I sit and read."

— C. S. Lewis, from *Reflections on the Psalms*

THOUGH WAR BREAK OUT

Blessed is he who meditates day and night.
Psalm 1:1-2

ASHERE

This time the collision wasn't fatal;
I knocked the doe off the road and backed up

to check. In my low beams, her head high,
those giant black eyes blinked slowly, confused.

Difficult this morning to concentrate
on the psalmic text — *Happy is the man*

whose delight is in the law of the Lord —
which feels irrelevant to everything

that has been flailing at my heart these days.
But how else to learn an answer for how

the tyranny of bleak appearances
drains the soul of all will to persevere?

He is a tree whose leaf does not wither.
I am like chaff that the wind blows away.

Be warned, you rulers of the earth.
Psalm 2:10

HARD TIMES

We wait out this blizzard at the far edge
of whatever suffering it may pile on

the less well kept. Easy for us to love
the bride-white beauty through our air-tight

windows or even brave the elements
one well-plowed mile for two-dollar coffees

at our favorite Zagat-rated café.
Never without a log for the fireplace,

we are thankful for our comforts – though we
sign contracts for these benefits insured

by policies that conspire against all
for whom there remains no room in the inn.

Easy to feel the innkeeper's bind
with the wind chill pushing twenty below.

May your blessing be on your people.
Psalm 3:8

AMONG THE LIVING

We lie down and sleep; and we wake again.
Like dying, or the way I wish it were.

The Lord gives to his beloved sleep, but
few care. Those who do I tend to welcome

as I do your eyes morning to morning.
Evening to evening, the pace picking up,

we lie down and sleep; we wake again,
our field of vision – blink – stroboscopic.

Blink again – we are surrounded by foes
who loathe our sloth, regard my love

to laze beside you of no benefit
to the commonweal. Which is true. So I

may quit my day job. What will they say then?
We lie down and sleep – and wake again.

How long, O men, will you love delusions and seek
false Gods?   Psalm 4:2

AGAINST SOLIPSISM

Is it unacceptably romantic
to say aloud that urban poetry

reads as if it needs to get out more, needs
more than a holiday in the country

to curb its solipsistic tendencies?
Most of the universe is — pause — nature.

Imagine hip-hop referring to plums
or an Ashbery knockoff ascending

into the euphony of coherence.
What makes sense of anything that happens

behind locked doors is that which has no need
of a door, real or metaphorical,

to upset one's cognitive apple cart.
Say, the slightest breeze beneath a doorjamb.

Their throat is an open grave.
Psalm 5:9

MOTO AT BROADWAY AND HEWES

— Brooklyn, NYC

Whatsoever is vulgar by design —
substandard housing, most packaged goods,

souls lacking virtuous aspiration,
anything ignoble or half-assed — will,

when the splendor appears, be swept up,
collected like so much rubbish, and burned.

Imagine earth's spirit clarified,
the good body set free from corruption.

Until then, there is music for voice
and double bass where fugitive hope

may find sanctuary, here and there cafés
serving nightly as temples of refuge.

When the splendor comes, who will not see it?
Whose knee will not bow or tongue confess?

My bones are in agony.
Psalm 6:2

DESIRE

I want to live where no one lies
to the suffering child who asks, "How long?" —

deceive a child, and she dies a little,
a little death, a little death, then gone —

and where every liar, ashamed, finally
turns from his duplicity, such a horn section

playing in the background as overcomes
the world, renews the earth, raises the dead —

which may mean heaven, but I am not prepared
to give up on the possibility here.

He who is pregnant with evil gives birth to
disillusionment.   Psalm 7:14

NARCISSUS POETICUS

unlike the heady air of paperwhites,
my slow, odoriferous return

to dust. We are full of what? *Shit* occurs
to me. And the Spirit would concur.

True, it is said when we pray, our words
are, to God, as incense. But how is this?

For they are rank with resistance
to the holy and with lust, their language

reeking with vengeance toward our enemies.
Deliver us, good Lord, from awful praying.

May the rhetorically repulsive be
removed to an air-tight composter.

Not so my blooming paperwhites. I enter
the apartment, inhale – and remember:

You have set your glory above the heavens.
Psalm 8:1

INSTRUCTIONS, WITH A QUESTION

On a clear dry night, assign the bright stars
proximity, the dim ones the greater

distances; give your sight time to adjust,
and the heavens will assume relative

dimension, seem to deepen.
Tell your high-minded scientific friends

to lighten up, get the picture: Milton's
winged Satan, hungry, descending from sphere

to sphere, eyeing the sparrow-brained and blind.
Humankind, that is. Lunch meat. Look again:

the moon and planets, stars and – it would seem –
nothing else. Good thing, bad thing? Nothing

we can do about it. Any number
of futures left wholly to us. And that glory!

Let the nations know they are but men.
Psalm 9:20

FORGET GOD

"It is natural to fight," he says, leaning
against the water cooler, the counselor's

room tight with suntanned boys, our chests showing.
His name is Jorge. He is from Mexico.

Later that night, he will also tell us
we do not know how to treat a woman.

This is not a movie. It is Tuesday,
we are all sixteen years old and looking

for a truth to try on like a boxer's robe.
(What is summer camp good for, if not this?)

Jorge's truth is pure silk – "Hermanos,
nature compels our defense of high ground" –

and we believe everything he says,
beginning, that night, with his eyes and grin.

His enemies are crushed, they collapse.
Psalm 10:10

THE WICKED MAN

Opening King David, the reader may
resist initially the heavy ink

against "the wicked man," dismiss the pitch
as rhetorically transparent, the cant

of every royal house, their fear showing.
This reader may also own a horse farm,

manage a hedge fund. Other readers –
think poor and disenfranchised, the wards

of insolvent nation-states – are without
hope in this heavy world, except one: God

will break the arms of all who hold themselves
beyond account. The wicked man is no

mere figure of speech. Ask the miserable.
They will tell you King David got it right.

When the foundations are being destroyed, what
can the righteous do?   Psalm 11:3

SNAPSHOT

Psalm 11, here's the picture: a god
who hates all purveyors of violence

and answers their mere bows and arrows with
an apocalyptic maelstrom. What I see:

a comedy – no laughing matter – where
the villains receive what they've intended

for their victims, who then inherit all
the thugs had planned for themselves. Think Esther.

But who gives a damn for any of this
or cares what it may mean? See there – outside

the window – the faithfulness of daybreak
slanting orange through a scrim of new snow.

Across all time zones, alarms are sounding.
Awakes the bitter heart's will to destroy.

We own our lips — who is our master?
Psalm 12:4

REASONS I WRITE

Those who assume they have no one
to whom they must account for their words,

like politicians, bankers, headmasters,
theologians, poets, older brothers —

they are wrong. *Every knee will bow, every*
tongue confess. So I do not use words

like "shit" or "Sovereign Lord" unaware.
Berryman — after Hopkins — wrote truly:

that line about Christ being the only
just critic. I write because it takes little

to spark my rage, and Saint Paul said we must
toil with our hands for the end of anger

is murder, and if any would be saved,
they must, with *fear and trembling*, work it out.

AMONG LUMINOUS THINGS

In this ocean of ordinary light,
we are reef dwellers. Whether brain coral

or parrot fish or moray, we all do
our bit, then die. The ocean teems entire,

a whole we believe by faith, wrestling
with the darkness and sorrow in our hearts.

I will never regard as wise the fool
who would have me slap a muzzle on

the voice within, small and still, inspiring
praise of whoever it may be who holds

all this in brilliant fullness. I say
let fly with adoration, thanks, and more,

for if this is not the deeper reason
we are here, then there is no reason.

God is present.
Psalm 14:5

SHORTSIGHTED

— for Bill, believer and photographer

You shoot the glorious — a crimson leaf
clinging to a bare branch, a snow-gray sky —

yet hanker for glory — that pure essence
of the uncreated Father of lights.

Though not one to say there is no God,
I am stuck on the quip about the bird

in hand being better than any two
that may be futzing about in the bush.

No doubt heaven's great, but this here's amazing.
Go ahead, call me shortsighted. It's true:

I'm happy camping in light's gallery
and praising the hard, full-spectrum effects

of here — now — ahead of me, a red fox
on the pond trail taking her own sweet time.

Lord, who may dwell in your sanctuary?
Psalm 15:1

EUCHARIST

Never have I felt a natural draw
to work anywhere close to an altar,

though, with this loose pile of sticks laid neatly
on a bare patch of earth, the ambition

to live quietly, minding my business,
becomes oblation, an ordinary

work of hands in service to grace. No priest
required, no victim, knife, or temple tax.

To this ground may a sweet, heavenly fire
descend. Here, where air sickens with the stench

of war and the perfunctory smoke
of religious ceremony, I turn –

keep us safe, O Lord, for you are our God –
to collect windfall for the coming night.

The sorrows of those will increase who run
after other gods.   Psalm 16:4

RUSH HOUR

I saw troops patrolling Grand Central,
teams of state police boarding all trains to

and from the universe. In the name of
Code Orange we station our gun-bearers

where and whenever we feel exposed.
On the train ride out, I drew attention

to a piece of luggage all by itself.
The porter assured me that the owner

had asked to put it there, but I worried
that the foreign-born porter was lying.

Is there nowhere safe? No sanctuary here?
Later, turning onto campus, I waved

to Sarge in his van keeping watch by night.
Not even the faithful....

As for the deeds of men —
Psalm 17:4

SHE SAID

Let the Spirit write the poems through you.
Yet the Spirit I know works in us as we

work on things like love – putting out the trash
without having to be reminded – which

I am very far from getting right. Poems
may serve love, but it would not be God's way

to bypass our humanity to make
texts pleasing to him. Otherwise they might

emerge in meadows like rocks urged up through
topsoil by freeze and thaw. To hell with poems.

What matters: some help with love, for we who
frame laws and build our flimsy arguments

resist at every turn the Spirit's work
and shut our hearts against the gentle friend.

He brought me out into a spacious place.
Psalm 18:19

SETH'S POND, WEST TISBURY

— All things hold together.
Colossians 1:17

Two lady's-slippers up along the path,
a kingfisher, the indifferent moon

still hanging in a brilliant, mid-spring sky,
my son in a sweater in a rowboat —

thank you. I choose to believe
the universe not merely big, but chock-full

with presence. Yet might the pessimist be
right about us — pitiable flecks of dust?

With terror in the air, the NBA
shifting into All-Star mode, and ninety

e-mails to clear by Monday, what is true?
(Why, O my soul, do you prattle on thus?)

A tall reed gives slightly in the cool breeze,
nearly buckles when a redwing alights.

Their voice goes out into all the earth.
Psalm 19:4

SO

If all created things speak wordlessly
of their creator – a turkey's wattle? –

then what do tax loopholes say about us?
Or bombed-out cities? The gossip of blue

highways – quaint, inaudible buzz – is it
praise or lamentation? Could even these

restless streams make glad the heart of God?
Old Madeline (*Wind in the Door*) L'Engle

says all true art, looking death in the face
and rising into light, feeds "the River."

O, to be able to hear, unfiltered,
the riotous vertical tongues of trees

and see beneath their cowled humility
the fire that burns yet will not consume them.

May the Lord send help from Zion.
Psalm 20:1-2

ANSWER ME

Bill's a friend, homeowner, married man – says
their small lakeside place has begun to feel

too much for them – can't seem to keep up with
what's breaking down – and back on campus

"well done" has become a moving target
he quit trying to hit months ago. No

surprise his wish to remain here has quit
on him – Donna starts round eight of chemo

next week. This morning my wife surprised me:
"If Bill decides to leave, we should leave, too."

What's left to keep us staying anywhere
when, despite faith, hope, love, we keep losing

ground to discouragement, the suspicion
that no amount of work will ever be enough?

Root out their seed from among the children of men.
Psalm 21:10

SHOCK AND AWE

Little words build up, become fighting words,
and before you know it, some enemy

has us believing our cause is righteous.
Which is when our poets, like prophets —

or sorely agitated roosters — take
courage and launch preemptory psalms,

smart bombs aimed at the heads of the wicked.
Pretty ugly stuff. Today, as I prayed

in a local wildlife sanctuary,
two kestrels rose from the meadow, hovered

like the Spirit above the primal sea,
and clarified my way forward. Holding

to beauty, I must leave the rest to others
who may not hear the word of April wings.

I am a worm and not a man.
Psalm 22:6

IN FACT

Show me an absolutely placid mind,
and I'll show you a corpse or one as good

as dead: one in denial of the swill –
the lies of desire – I keep falling for.

Try as we may, we cannot lift ourselves
from ourselves rabbit-from-hat-like and live

to tell of it, though liars make bundles
claiming otherwise. We are a mess, yet

it pleases Him – and let us quit whining
about the gender of divinity –

to be numbered among the conflicted.
So here, among yappy dogs, snorting bulls,

bone-thin cows, let us offer God our praise:
Damn, you're beautiful; and your handiwork.

The Lord is my shepherd.
Psalm 23:1

23

Roger loathes being likened to a sheep,
struggles with self-esteem, takes the figure

as an affront to his intelligence.
Arlys loves Roger, so when the preacher

went on for twenty minutes about sheep,
the Shepherd, and the sheep pen, Arlys winced

and prayed for Roger. Prayed he would not want
to walk home alone, cancel their outing

to the state park, return to the city.
Arlys loves God, believes Roger's doubting

could be turned to confidence overnight.
If only he would hear the Shepherd's voice,

she would sleep beside him in the fold, lack
nothing, anoint his head with oil. *Amen.*

Lift up your heads, O you gates; be lifted up, you ancient doors.
Psalm 24:7

CROSSING THE WILLIAMSBURG BRIDGE

— Easter morning

Walt Whitman's Brooklyn behind us, we are walking
to Manhattan and a late brunch in Chinatown:

steamed dumplings, rooster sauce, pan-fried sesame bread,
plastic bowls of spicy mushroom soup, oolong tea.

We walk above traffic, the river, beside the JMZ line,
share elevated pedestrian lanes with cyclists, Hassidim,

speed walkers, hippies, Latinos, arty types in all black.
You are here — a mantra learned from maps on kiosks

in suburban malls — plays in my head, and softly (to myself)
I offer up an Easter hymn under Jerusalem-blue skies.

All families will bow before him; he is the King of glory.
To the south, a thin column of cloud rises like altar smoke.

The earth is the Lord's, and the fullness thereof.
In this light, even the jaded skyline stands transfigured.

He instructs sinners in his ways.
Psalm 25:8

WITH BILL AT BAFFLIN SANCTUARY

We walk woodland trails cut by volunteers
and kid about total depravity

which, pertaining to salvation, translates
even "the greatest geniuses are blind-

er than moles." The path is soft underfoot,
the laurel late-blooming. Beside a pond

he unpacks his camera. Can a snapshot
reveal the affliction of our nature?

I take refuge under translucent leaves,
leave him to his patient compositions.

But what's the point? His kind wife is dying,
and he has left the house to take pictures

of ferns uncurling. Do I hear myself?
Are they not – forgive me – portraits of her?

Test me, O Lord, and try me.
Psalm 26:2

GENERAL CONFESSION

In each promise of faithfulness, traces
of countless betrayals: averted eyes,

a voice's tremor. Like the air we breathe
or the glances we exchange with strangers

on strobe-lit dance floors, we test positive
for impurity. But do not expect

a list of lurid details in these lines;
I am neither Catholic nor Lowell nor Plath.

I am merely — how does the song go — "prone
to wander." So have we any chance,

this side of heaven, at a constant heart?
Or even modest progress toward that end?

The word's out: *love covers a multitude*
of sins. Is this the best we can hope for?

I will see the goodness of the Lord in the land
of the living.   Psalm 27:13

TO SELF-PITY

What a force you are! Cyclonic, godlike,
irresistible as lust is irresistible, and thick

with generations of flung wreckage, blunt
as thugs. Who, coracled in mere feeling,

can stand against such compelling torque?
I confess: you are a familiar ride, a drug

of choice, a sluttish changeling, your blouse
half-unbuttoned, eyes fierce with loathing.

Where, in my soul's fluid world, currents
meet, there, turning on the slightest axis

of an insecurity, you – siren vortex –
draw me into your sweet, insatiable self.

Old friend and nemesis, there, too, a Rock
of refuge may be found. To Him I will cleave.

Be their shepherd and carry them forever.
Psalm 28:9

NO WORRIES

— for my tour guide at the interview

We take them as they come, ages twelve
to nineteen, dress them in blue blazers, and run

them ragged. We get away with it because
their parents worry, and the lawns are presidential.

If we do one thing well it is attending
to the millions of surfaces that present themselves

to a visitor's eye at each turn along
the arcing, neatly bordered pathways. All this

beneath broad, heavy-leafed trees not native
to this corner of the state: copper beech,

ginkgo, weeping red maple. We are a world apart,
not entirely unto ourselves, just safely to one side.

But it was not the brick dorms or landscaping,
the dress code or college list that drew me

twenty years ago to these lawns, this life decked
with adolescents. It was the canvas hammock

you said most visitors never see slung across
the stream – between two birches – behind the rink.

Fall and spring, you and your friends would go there
and one at a time climb into the heavy cotton, pull

the frayed sides up across your chests and swing,
companions pumping the ropes for you, and all the way

to the top you'd turn, face nothing but the water
beneath you, then over you'd go – again

and again – wrapped in the weathered chrysalis.
I cannot say exactly what it was about that

late April afternoon that won me over to the job,
but I will be ever grateful for the detour.

The God of glory thunders.
Psalm 29:3

NEIGHBOR AS THEOLOGIAN

How can she talk about a "word from God"?
The weather, yes, or the fate of our hedge.

A snake or the shrinking odds of her spouse
beating cancer, sure. But a word from God?

As though God were an actual person,
albeit incomprehensibly vast.

Yet this is how she talks, the way I talk
about my son from whom I could never

hear too much or too often, who's only
hours away in Brooklyn. Why, unless

my sin were envy, would I begrudge her
an assurance of contact? More likely,

I long for what she has, embarrassed, pained
by my lack of openness to mystery —

which, she has told me, is wholly present
in, with, and under the hedge between us.

When you hid your face, I was dismayed.
Psalm 30:7

AS IT IS

The face of God is hidden from me.
I see only old walls, the clutter

of familiar rooms – shelves of books, snapshots,
mix-and-match decor. Awake or asleep

and dreaming, no divine shook-foil glimmer
for my inmost eye. Rumors reach me

of others' encounters – glimpses of His face –
but after devouring these, the want

remains. Is there some special training I need?
Last week a friend confided that for years

the Holy Ghost has shimmered inside her,
every moment beatific. My resolve:

to pretend my friend is not a liar
or schizophrenic – and to seek new friends.

He showed his wonderful love to me when I was
in a besieged city.   Psalm 31:21

PUTTING A NAME TO THE FACE

In Madagascar or Peru, St. Kitts
or Tasmania, wherever children,

despite all suffering, find games to play
or halt play to marvel at a column

of clouds collecting on some horizon;
wherever anyone takes care to make

ready a back room for a visitor –
sweep the floor for the ten-thousandth time,

place a fresh flower on the pillow – there
a glimpse, the face you know you know

in a crowd of strangers who disappears
before you get a fix on the distance

between you –
                    mercy! –
                                and that face.

Do not be like the horse or the mule which have
no understanding.   Psalm 32:9

BROTHER CHRONOS

Radio-controlled and programmed to check
in every four hours with an atomic

device deep in some bunker in Denver,
my travel clock is more monk than truant

on probation, for it desires correction,
six times a day turns outward toward the big

unseen world – receives it – then turns back
to serving my fascination with time.

No alarm or trumpet sounds to signal
the connecting moment – its mute faithfulness

wholly independent of audience –
and I would be its disciple, pray the hours,

live, contented, in step with the Spirit,
but my program is a prison named fear.

Still, how wonderful to know what time it is,
precise to within a millionth of a second.

From heaven the Lord looks down and sees
all mankind.   Psalm 33:13

REPORT

I flavor my food with long suffering.

The clothes in my closet are unironed.

I have never spoken in another tongue.

Given the option, I would work alone

or in the tested company of friends.

I find nothing holy in national

holidays though love getting the hours

off, time being the skin I look forward

to shedding once I am done with my life.

Between Eden and the New Earth, only

wind, music, and diligence feel at all

familiar. Here, everywhere is exile.

I will continue to speak this language.

Every word, a stand against losing heart.

GOD

Are all theophobic? No one wants to
be reminded. No thought, sentence, or deed

can escape the chill of divine review.
Dread being a dark matter of the soul,

engines of suppression hum constantly
flooding the wakeful mind with distractions

grand as virtue, common as relatives.
(How else to prevent the unwanted Word's

indelicate meaning from causing hurt?)
Judgment by one's peers can be useful, but

keep at bay the cool scrutiny of God
lest "luv" lose its warm inclusivity,

"my truth" its fragile singularity.
No "truth," though lovely, will be left standing

on the day Truth absolutely arrives.
Poor, middle class, rich; straight or gay – no one

questions the myth: autonomy, each one's
rule is law. But those who *fear the Lord* and

seek Him *lack nothing*, their fear a spring-fed
tributary to perfect freedom where

unruly wills find rest in serving Him.
Voice-beyond-language (still, small, holy),

wickedness reveals itself resisting
(xenophobically) Thy sovereign wisdom.

Yesterday, today, tomorrow – folly's
zero swallows her dreary children whole.

I will give thanks in the great assembly.
Psalm 35:18

WORD PROBLEM

They sit facing him in three rows, each row elevated six
inches above the one in front of it, and on each tier,
three narrow curved tables. In the first row sit four
conferees per table, in the second five, and the third six.
Looking at them from the lectern, he counts
forty-five in all – not one familiar or getting any
younger – though if he hadn't known in advance he'd
have never guessed it was a roomful of fifty-one year
olds. He makes forty-six, and as he looks at them, he
thinks of each as a mirror and calmly studies his
response to every different tie, chin, nose, hairline, as if
sitting before him were as many versions of himself as
populate his unconscious and this were a summit of
selves. The topic: a spiritual cost/benefit analysis of the
respective merits of reading, aerobic exercise, and
contributing to the commonweal, with narrative
implications for both the good life and dying well. Why
else would forty-five busy fifty-one year olds agree to
gather in this three-tiered conference room? Why else
would he be addressing them?

*The evildoers lie fallen — thrown down, not
able to rise.*   Psalm 36:12

TWO WORLDS

1

From multinational corporations
to international regulatory agencies,

from rogue states and terror cells
to the holy democratic empire —

behind it all, a clever, loose alliance
of "powers and principalities" fueling

fires more terrible than Mordor's.
Has anyone an oracle against this world?

By what spirit would the sayer speak?
Would he wrap himself in vestments

and deliver prophecies like a saint?
Or strap on a hissing Telecaster,

step to the microphone, and rip the tops
off the heads of all who fear nothing

but their own loss of say in how
the business of this world gets done.

2

There is another world – where Orion,
like an older brother, drops by each year

on my October birthday, and the glory
of the cosmos is all signal, no noise.

Here the mountains we walk among rise
from pristine fiords, each silver river

a sacrament by which we and all things
thrive side by side; day or night

no clever snake or shadow deceives. Here
the prayers of all those waylaid

by the first world and left behind for dead
have found their audience; faith knows

what may not be confirmed. So it is
two worlds inhere. The one I love: a vast,

endless miracle in super-slow-mo
extending through and beyond Nike.

Consider the blameless.
Psalm 37:37

IN MINISTRY

We dress for the job, learn to speak right,
when required, employ polysyllabics.

Yet what's to keep us from being found out?
We are a field of splendid grasses

soon to vanish like smoke from a ruin.
How we strive to gain the dominical inch

we know will guarantee our future.
Ah, to be revered by generations!

And I am straining in that same field
for that same reward. O Lord, have mercy.

Send us help to hear and make sense of
your ancient laughter – unstop our ears –

and then – why not – a specialist to offer
in-service workshops in humility.

I have become like a man whose mouth can offer no reply.
Psalm 38:14

ON SILENCE, BRIEFLY

— for Barry Moser, artist and teacher

Fifteen, winter term,

we arrive early, no noise
but him breathing through his beard,

his pen's thin metal quill skating across the rough ice
of handmade rag paper,

a broad-lipped lady's-slipper emerging.

You are the one who has done this.
Psalm 39:9

LORD

Get off my back. For a season
obsess over another's
imperfection.
With you constantly
reviewing my little existence,
what shot have I at joy?
Your beauty
amplifies my homeliness.
How I long to sing before I die,
but as your project
I have become a mute
phantom pacing.
Is it so wicked to want a little
rest for my soul? Behold
what your scrutiny
works in me: heaviness of heart,
ceaseless introspection;
with your eye upon me –
noble moth
that I amount to – all hope
has flown. What are
a man's chances against the prince
of righteousness? Please,

take a break. Book
a holiday cruise to elsewhere.
At the very least,
listen to my cry, O God:
Look away from me,
that I may rejoice again
before I depart and am no more.

Happy the man who does not trust in such as go
about with lies.   Psalm 40:4

CROSSING THE NOTCH

— for Deb

In tight, fast-wicking garb and hiking boots,
he looked like someone who would know

how much farther we had
to where the Long Trail met the notch road,

so when he told us we were nowhere
near and would need to retrace our slow

steps back up and across the icy ridge,
our sweat-soaked cotton clothes grew heavier.

Knees failing us, even the light breeze
of a late-October mid-afternoon became

an enemy plotting our ruin, and in that
trail-side exchange, our hike

revealed itself as pure folly, potentially dire.
Who, O Lord, is not a novice, an amateur

in this business of setting out and arriving?
So progress came down to a bushwhacker's

word versus the weakened faith of flatlanders
in the cryptic text on a trailhead sign

and occasional glimpses of thin white blazes.
Finally, we pushed by him

and, inside a descending hour, found
ourselves – despite the grand indifference

of a shadowless day in northern Vermont –
safely on the narrow road through the notch.

Blessed is he who has regard for the weak.
Psalm 41:1

AMEN AND AMEN

When Cory told me how a friend's daughter,
from the fifth floor of a hotel along the route,

sent the entire dark-suited security phalanx
of a presidential motorcade into a mad scramble

by her unladylike middle finger raised in protest,
I wondered where I was, what year, what country.

Then I read an interview with a retired general
speculating that the detonation of a WMD

on these shores would spark a wholesale scrapping
of both the Constitution and Bill of Rights,

and thirty difficult years of putting history behind me
dissolved, the scene changed, the woods out back

suddenly defoliated, a rank odor fouled the air.
How long had I been asleep? I am stunned

with the burden of my countless accommodations
to denial. Show mercy, O Christ, and preserve

my heart's freedom to see and honor the beauty
of your hand in all things good, right, and true.

Renew the faith of that angry daughter.
Even as shadows lengthen inevitably toward

the darkness when no one can work, strengthen
my knees that I may not falter along the way

that leads through the valley of terror.
In this present — wherever we are, whatever

year it may be — raise up an unconquerable chorus
of resistance and praise, from everlasting to everlasting.

NOTES

On the First Sunday in Advent 2002, this project began: to make a slow, contemplative read (*lectio divina*) through the Bible's *Book of Psalms*, one psalm a week, and by the week's end to draft a poem bearing an impression, however subtle, of the biblical text, with influence also from my surroundings – local to cosmological – and from whatever may have been of personal importance that week – lived or invented. Three horizons, one poem a week; I've fallen a little off the pace, but my intention remains to struggle with the dailiness of the work and write my way through the Psalter. In the end, there will be, Lord willing, four books in a series entitled *Opening King David*.

Though I set for myself no formal parameters, I found pleasure early on in ten-syllable lines and fourteen line poems. Regarding epigraphs and biblical quotations: I borrow / adapt chiefly from the New International Version of the Bible, with occasional glances at the King James Version and the 1928 *Book of Common Prayer*. The following notes may not be necessary or illuminating, but here they are:

Psalm 1   *Ashere* is Hebrew for "blessed" or "happy." The italicized lines are from the psalm, though I take modest liberties. Had the car been an older model, it would have been totaled.

Psalm 5   "Moto" (as in Moto Guzzi) is the name of a favorite café-restaurant under the elevated JMZ line on the border between the Latino and Hassidic neighborhoods of South Williamsburg. As is the case in many of these poems, this one contains echoes of several New Testament passages: *Philippians 4:8, Revelation 21:1-4, Philippians 2:6-11.*

Psalm 7   *Narcissus Poeticus* is the name of a small, white, aromatic daffodil I have always known as the paperwhite. Again, a New Testament echo: *Revelation 8:1-5.*

Psalm 8   In *Paradise Lost*, the descent of Milton's Satan to earth through the celestial spheres cul-minates in his lighting, vulture-like, on a tree in Eden. Purely fanciful, Milton's description makes cinematic the unseen entrance of that deceitful shape-shifter into the human exper-ience.

Psalm 11   The biblical *Book of Esther*, though hardly funny, is a classic comedy: in the end, the bad guy (Haman) gets the misery he planned for the good guy (Mordecai), and the good guy gets the glory the bad guy had intended for himself.

Psalm 12   The italicized words are from *Philippians 2:9-13* (New Testament), and the Hopkins line about Christ being the just critic is lifted from poem "10" of John Berryman's *Eleven Addresses to the Lord* in LOVE & FAME.

Psalm 16   "turning onto campus" – In 1986 I moved onto the grounds of a boarding school; since then, all trips home have been toward and back onto campus.

Psalm 19   "the fire that burns yet will not consume them"
                  cf. *Exodus 3:1-6.*

Psalm 21   "like the Spirit above the primal sea" – cf.
                  Genesis 1:1-2.

Psalm 22   "numbered among the conflicted" is meant to
                  echo the messianic prophesy in *Isaiah 53:12*
                  regarding the Suffering Servant: "he was
                  numbered among the transgressors." The
                  italicized last line is my summary of the psalm's
                  last six verses, with a nod to *Psalm 8.*

Psalm 24   Line 11 is a conflation of *Psalm 22:27* and *Psalm
                  24:10.* Line 14 is from *Psalm 24:1.*

Psalm 25   The quotation in lines 4 and 5 is from John
                  Calvin's *Institutes of Religion* (Book II, Chapter
                  2, Section 18).

Psalm 26   "prone to wander" – I have sung a spiritual
                  song with this line, but I remember neither
                  the tune nor any other words. The "word"
                  referred to in the last two lines is from *1 Peter
                  4:8* in the New Testament.

Psalm 30   "divine shook-foil glimmer" – cf. G. M.
                  Hopkins' "God's Grandeur," line 2; his
                  influence is everywhere in me if not in the
                  poems.

Psalm 33   "the New Earth" – cf. *Revelation 21:1.*

Psalm 34   The Hebrew psalm is an acrostic; the verses
            begin with successive letters of the alphabet.
            Each line of my poem does the same.

Psalm 35   As a math student, I hated word problems. This
            prose poem began as a vividly remembered
            dream.

Psalm 36   "powers and principalities" – In biblical
            theology, the nations and all earthly insti-
            tutions are understood as being players in
            humanity's rebellion against the sovereignty of
            God. This rebellion is fed by both human
            sinfulness and, as the 1979 *Book of Common
            Prayer* (p. 302) says, "Satan and all the spiritual
            forces of wickedness that rebel against God."
            In the New Testament, "powers and princi-
            palities" may be understood as angelic orders
            that rank very highly among these spiritual
            forces. "Mordor" is, of course, J. R. R. Tolkien's
            hellish invention in THE LORD OF THE
            RINGS. A Telecaster is a Fender electric guitar
            (and my axe of choice).

Psalm 40   "the notch" is Smugglers Notch, and that far
            north in Vermont the Long Trail is more prim-
            itive and rigorous than we expected.

Born and weaned in southern California, Brad Davis moved north to British Columbia at six weeks of age. Since 1980 and graduation from seminary in Pittsburgh, he has served in universities, schools, and churches in several states. In 1995 he received an MFA from Vermont College, and these days he directs The Writers Studio and teaches creative writing at Pomfret School in Connecticut, where he and his wife Deb, a jazz vocalist, have been on the faculty since 1987. Their son John, a professional musician in New York City, has provided his parents countless opportunities to escape to the big city to enjoy the clubs of Manhattan's Villages and the restaurants of Brooklyn's Williamsburg. Brad's reading venues include the Sunken Garden Poetry Festival and Oxford University; his work has appeared in *The Paris Review, Poetry, Michigan Quarterly Review, Puerto del Sol, Tar River Poetry, Ascent, The Anglican Review,* and other journals. He has received an AWP Intro Journal Award as well as several Pushcart nominations. Recently his chapbook, *Short List of Wonders*, was selected by Dick Allen for the 2005 Sunken Garden Poetry Prize.

For discussion and writing suggestions
that will increase your engagement
with *Though War Break Out*
visit the seminar page
of the Antrim House website:
www.antrimhousebooks.com

To order Antrim House titles
contact the publisher at

Antrim House
P.O. Box 111
Tariffville, CT 06081
860-217-0023
www.antrimhousebooks.com
eds@antrimhousebooks.com